# SPEECHES TO PLANTS AND ANIMALS

Christopher M Doyle

*To Amanda, Sam, Tom and Ruby*
*I think of you - and the rest is easy x*

*My heads swimming with poetry and prose...*

LLOYD COLE

# CONTENTS

# PREFACE

This is a collection of my poetry and prose. The first part of the book contains a selection of the poems written over the last thirty years or so.

Writing poems has always been - for me - a way to make sense of the contents of my head. Each one relates specifically to either something that has happened to me, something I maybe saw on the news - or an event in someone elses life.

The second part of the book is a section containing various chapter ones for ideas I have had over the years. The whole story for each remains locked inside my head alongside a little hope that one day I will write the rest of the story.

For now though, they are what they are. Incomplete, unfinished and barely begun.

I hope you enjoy reading them all.

Thank you
Chris

# POEMS

# ALL DISCO

Guest book guest list
Turned up late a party
Missed choked up
Spaced out throw
Some shapes getting
Out zoned in eyes closed
Bitten lip broken nose
He knows she's known
Outgoing ingrown
Fast pulse breath race
Hide here in case
Crouch down curl there
Punctured eyes
Little square
This scene doesn't mean
A thing. A thing. A thing. A thing.
Know less. Torn dress
Bloody knees cough
Please Sick hair stuck
There don't care isn't
Fair. Nothing is. So free
Sweating greatly
We will be
Hurts now didn't then
Take a breath start
Again. Be mean be man
Be mean.

# I AM JUST A FATHER

I used to dream of dragons
Wrote poems on the sun
Now I am just a Father
And you are just my son.
Take away my doubts Son
Be unto me a shield
Protect me as I cover you
And teach me when to yield
I used to harbour visions
Ambitious to the cause
Now I am a Father
And the world can see my flaws.
You are the thief of my ambition
I am the holder of your dream
I am content to watch you grow
I have lost the need to scheme.
I used to dream of grandeur
I thought each day of fame
Now I want the simpler things
For you to call my name.
The dragons and the sunshine
That lived inside my head
Now dance inside your heart and eyes
They live with you instead.

# OUTGUNNED

Keep moving. It's just fighting
Remembering to breathe
Dodging. Just reacting.
Don't think. Just be.
No planning. No aim.
Tick off another day.
One step.
Two step.
Baby steps.
You can't run.
You are thinking and you shouldn't
You think there is control
To be had
Just surrender.
Stop trying
Stop moving
Duck down behind the tall trees
And hide.
Be unseen
When your breath comes panting
And sweat pools in the
Small of your back
Hair sticking to your face
Just be.
They ARE coming
You are outgunned
And misdirected
They WILL catch you

CHRISTOPHER M DOYLE

# And it will NOT be pleasant

# SIX MINUTES

Something like a sonic scream pierces me
A fragile lament for my ears only
Hurtles through the sorrow
Burns hearts and turns minds
Of strangers even though
They don't hear its aching whisper.
Crossing mountains, it melts then splinters their brutal peaks
Cataclysmic landfalls and hurricanes are brought about.
It blazes sky-trails through the laden clouds
Effervescent it hurtles
Tearing worlds apart as it flies
Inexorably onwards from its point of departure
Your heart to mine
I hear your call from where I am
I respond as my heart thuds against my ribs
Like some fucking prisoner
With broken bloody fists he beats
Against the endless dark
Panting as my breath crystallises in the air
I hear your sonic sorrow and see
That no one else has heard
Only I
Only me your heart can call
Decades apart
Light years hence
You weep fat angry tears
That salt upon your lips
Believing I do not know

Perhaps I've forgotten
How to care. But you can just see
Deep in the dusty corners of your mind
Where even spiders will not go
That doubt and hate know to fear us
And I will return to you and hold you
And you know this, when I am there
All will be well.

# CURVES WITH DESTINATIONS

Trace a line
with the softest part
Of you
Destinations unknown
The undiscovered
Valley
But there
There is glory
A new sensation
Alien. Feels
Wrong to feel
Like this.
Soft pressure pushes back
Urging on for more
More urgent
Harder
And deeper, so much
Deeper
With frantic scrabbling
And tearing
All the while
More ardour
and
Harder until
It culminates
With joy and

Light and
Maybe.
Just
Sometimes
A hint
Of regret.

# SAMUEL

This is love
And nothing can come close
To how you make me feel
You make the sunshine real
And colours all seem brighter than they ever did before.
This is true love
I know because you said so
And it weakens me it makes me so afraid
But I know I've got it made
Because there's no doubt in my heart
This is the very start
Of a lifetime of devotion
And you can never do me wrong.
When I'm not with you
Your voice is in my head
You bring me succour
You alleviate the dread
This is hopeless
I cannot think when you are near
But your departure is the very thing I fear
You are my son
You've made me come alive
And when you hold me
I feel that I could thrive.
If I have a bad day
When everyone conspires
I know that when I see you
You'll greet me with a smile

CHRISTOPHER M DOYLE

This is perfection
and nothing can come near
I feel real love now I dared not think it true
How alive I am and it's all thanks to you.

# ON DAYS LIKE THESE

It should be raining when
You hear bad news. There
should be
thunder
and
lightning
and howling spiteful wind crashing things into other things.
The world should stop
Stop (at least for a minute or two)
Then
Carry on, the moment
Marked some how
People should pause and breathe
Each other in. They should
Hold Hands
And Kiss each other
Deeply. Without
Knowing quite why
They should be
Sad but not know
Why. Just that
Someone or something
Somewhere
Has gone.
Inwards or
Outwards – I don't
Know.
Become a little

less Orderly. Less here.
They should feel
What he felt. A tenth
A quarter. A third. And
Moving on, be grateful
That they did not feel the whole.

# HE DOES NOT KNOW
# WHICH WAY TO GO

He does not know which way to go
Which corner turned
Will bring freedom
The browning grass killed
By endless pissing
Men with guns
On the corner where
These children broke and
Fell. those daughter's torn
And damaged.
The light
Burned out of them by
A hundred cackling drunken Guns.
Broken glass crunches.
The dark turns into
Day light and thunder and
The shadows laugh and Murmur.
They stretch and
Curl and grow. There is Movement.
The moment will be unkind, he knows.
Breathlessly
He takes the route unknown.
Pooling sweat prickles his neck
He tastes their tears.
He sees their
Faces bruised and broken

# He does not know which way to go

# THE BOX

Just three feet long this box I hold
How light this box should be
What lies within I loved the most
This box sat on my knee
Just 20 steps I carry it
This box just two foot wide
What lies within I loved the most
The weight that is inside
It's heavier that I had thought
The box I lay to rest
Earth will warm the one I love
I hold it to my chest.
My steps are stumbling as I walk
I near the gaping ground
Although I weep and scream and curse
The box will hear no sound.

# SHIFT/DELETE

Shift/delete
Are you sure
Ok
Ok
Blue line grows
Slows and
Falters.
System error this file is in use
It cannot be deleted
This memory remains
Ingrained on the chip
Burned in
A ghost file
ZERO ONE ONE 010010010000001101100110 ONE ONE ONE
ONE
01110110011001010010000001111001011011110111 0101
01110000011011000110010101100001011100110110010100
1 ZERO ZERO ZERO ZERO 00110100001100101011011 0001 ONE
ONE 0000001000000110110101100101
01101001001000000110000101101101001000000 ONE ONE
ONE 0011011011110111001001110010 0111 ONE ZERO 01
Shift/delete
Attempt 2 of 2
Attempt failed
Reboot. Reboot.

# GROUND LEVEL

When something that
Is nothing Happens and
My teeth vibrate and
Grind, I can only think
Of her. Of him and him.
When my skin begins to crawl
And a dark cloud gathers.
When I see that number still
In my phone. When I open
Doors best left
Closed and bolted and barred
I think of them. The three.
When my breath comes
In gasps and shudders
Shallow and quick
And I
Start to look inside
Where nothing
Good can
Be.
I close my eyes and
Picture them each
In fine and intricate
Detail.
I think of them.
The rest is easy.

# DESTROY ME WITH AN ATOM BOMB

Destroy me with an atom bomb
Flay my skin – put out my sun
Burn my palms – tear out my hair
Blind me so you are not there

Break my spine and make me crawl
Shoot me dead against a wall
Hold me under – make me drown
Fill my lungs and fill my mouth

Eviscerate me with a stare
Cut out my Tongue – I do not care
Emasculate me with a blade
Crush-kill-destroy the world I've made

Crush my hopes and steal my gold
Kill my youth and make me old
Crease my skin and turn me grey
Ruin me in your own way

Hurl me to the stratosphere
The edge of death then pull me near
Say you're sorry and then smile
Say you'll stop just for a while

Give me hope then crush it too
Seal eyes and mouth with superglue
Annihilate me with a sneer

Make me cry and show me fear

Suffocate me every night
Just to teach me you are right
Black and decker through my brains
Corrupt and harm my dead remains

Do all the things you want to do
Do all you need but when you're through
Treat me to a knowing smile and
Let me know you'll stay a while.

# THE CONSTANT

Dream of rivers and of oceans
Speak in tongues of diamond skies
Be forever in my heart
Be with me till our love dies.
Travel far or stay by my side,
Whichever, you are always near.
I feel your trust and I feel rested,
As in your arms I know
no fear.
Shed from your heart your baseless doubts,
And trust in all I say or do.
Believe in this, the only constant,
In all my dreams and thoughts and actions,
I see, my dear, only you.

# LOOKING FROM
# A HILLTOP

It is the grinnnnnnnnnding of the teeth
The bzzzzzzzzing of the head
Like jonny 5 I short
Cir
Cir
Circircir
Cccccccccccccc
Iiiiiiiiiii iiiii iiiii iiiiii
.......
.......
........
Come to.
Then recollect.
What have I
Said/thought/done
The sense there he is waiting
There he is. What? Why?
I CAN SEE him
..... ......
Bzzzzzzzzzzz
Four days without......
Grrrrr
Eye eye eye
nnnnndddddnnnnnggg
Guh guh guh
Why can't you

CHRISTOPHER M DOYLE

Why can't you
Why can't you
Fucking
See.

# INTERRUPTED COMMS

This line is broken.
I can't HEAR YOU.
Buzz. Crackle.
Brrrrrrrrrrrrrr.
I wish you could hear me.
Interference on the cable
Crossed lines.
Impedence.
Sorry caller
Your message was not recei…
Nor underst..d
Dddddddddddddd
Some echo?
Hang up and redial
Cssssssshhhhhhhhh
Please repeat.
White noise drowns voices.
This line is.

# TRIED SEMAPHORE

tried semaphore
Tried semaphore
Flags would not flutter when
There was no breeze
Stood on the roof
Of my house and shouted
slipping on slates in the rain
No one looked up
Clumsy hands no use for
Signing hung loosely at my side
So
I tapped out a .-. .... -.-- .... DASH
Made no .... . -. .... . to any— -DOT .
Poured out all .. / .- —
.... .-. — -.- . / — -DOT .-.. -.- / DASH .DOT DOT. . / – .-. ... – ....
.. / .- — / ... — .-. .-. -.- / .. / -. . . -.. / .... . .-.. -. / .. / .- — / DOT DOT
DOT – .-. ..- –. DASH DASH. .-.. .. -. -. / .- .. – .... / – .... / -.. .- -.- / – — /
-.. .- -.-
I / DASH DOT DOT DOT -.. / — -.- / ..-. .-. .. . -. . -..

# NOT TODAY

Say what you will, my dear,
Curse me to the day,
As hard as you may rein me in,
Further I will stray.
The world is full of prettiness,
And you are simply plain,
You know that when I see her face,
I do not know your name.
Eclipsed you are by anyone,
Marooned upon the moon,
I try so hard to leave you, dear,
The day is coming soon.
I will not be tethered, dear,
I will not be held down,
And when I look at other girls
You will not make a sound.
Hold still your acid tongue, my dear,
And look the other way,
Although I speak of leaving you,
It will not be today.

# WE ARE FROM THE TIME BEFORE

We are from the time before
Ones and zeroes were
Nothing or more
Just numbers
Just numbers
We saw the advent of machines
In code
We saw
The digital age begin
We knew the before
And we knew the after
And shaped what came between
Remember us – your fathers
And your mothers
In the before we dug the ground
We turned the wood
We scaled the hills
And cleared the paths
As yet untrodden
In the after we wrote
In basic words that shaped
Things. In spritely movement
We edged onto your screens
With simple notes and sounds
We knew the before
We knew the after

We made the in between
We are the Oppenheimers.

# BULLETS BURST

When all the planets
Are aligned and the
Stars start to burn
If forests start to smoulder
And deep rivers turn
To ice. When worlds
Turn on their axis
And the dark night
Shines like sunlight
If the dead return to living
And the clocks turn
Slowly back
If bullets burst from
Barrels and then turn
Into fragrant blooms
And in turn, ignite
And burn and fly
Then
And only then
Will I forget you.

# DEPRESSION

"You're an ugly motherfucker" rang the bells,
As I stumbled fell and screamed through all my hells,
Sixteen layers to the depths of my despair,
Just emptiness lies waiting for me there.
I fell before, but that was not this far or bad,
Because before I only felt a little sad,
But this time I cannot see how I can climb,
Out of this darkness to the distant light that shines.
Don't try to tell or show me what I have achieved,
Because this darkness gives me all I want or need,
I am enshrouded in the depths of my despair,
And I know that deep inside that you don't care.
Blackness falling, night is calling,
Calling me to rest,
If I choose so, just let me go
I feel it's for the best.

# HOLD IT

Hold it
Tight in your hand
Look at me
And tell me
Eyes wide
It's the best thing in the world
Move slowly
Tightening your grip
Eye contact
All the time
Be here
Just here
Just hold it
Tell me where
I should put my hands
Just once
Just once
Say you understand

# WHEN WE HELD HANDS

When we held hands I
Felt soft and gentle flesh
Press lightly on mine
I felt everything. I said
Nothing.
I stood to attention and
Did not waver once.
You, however, looked
Around and up and down
Then, looking through me,
Briefly tightened your grip
Looked downwards and then
Let go.

# DO NOT FORGET
# YOUR DYING KING

Do not forget your dying king
Reiterate his name
Recall the night that covered you
That creeps this way again
Believe in your own majesty
The gift he gave to you
The simple rhymes he wrote in code
That blessed you with the truth
Forget about his feeble frame
The things he cannot do
Concentrate on how he was
And what he gave to you
The cruelty of morning and
The hate he took away
Follow his example still
And keep the night at bay
Do not forget your Dying King
His lessons or his name
Forget the night that covered you
The legacy remains

# WILL YOU FIND ME

Will you find me hidden there
Inside the folds and curves
Of folded fabric.
You thought me lost - scattered
Elsewhere but I lay here
In patience and with fortitude
I linger. Waiting in the darkness
For that tiny shard of light
For the motes that will curl and dance
Displaced by reaching fingers
Blindly grasping with groaning
And exasperated sighs.
Alone and silent with these
Fragments torn and crumpled
I did not hide here purposefully
I was forgotten that is all
My purpose is purposeless
Whilst I wait
For the answer to
The question - will you find me.

# DUST THIS HEART FOR FINGERPRINTS

Dust this heart for fingerprints
A chalked outline on the floor
Marks the spot where he fell
Frozen there in time
Shaking hands touch it
Exposed. Open. Scalpel slides.
Smoothly and clinically excising
All detritus until all there is
Is what there is
A heart that beats a most
Unique rhythm. That dances
And leaps
To its own tune.
When magnified by ten thousand
Look. See what there is to see
This heart.
Covered in layer upon layer
Take care and redraw the lines
Scuffed by the onlookers
Look closely at these fingerprints
They are not his. They are not mine.

# THESE THINGS COME IN THREES (THEY SAY)

These things come in threes
(They say)
From three sides
Closing in
Slowly and without care for
How it makes him feel
Behind them is some sunlight
But that too is fading
And drawing in to leave
The night.
We weep inside for the
Small boy who cannot
See or comprehend
What this is
This unjust unfairness
Like armour on the skin
These things that come in threes
(they say)
Draw in and in
Enclosing him
Covering him
Until all there is
Is a singular view
Facing forwards
Through a visor slit
In a suit of cold cruelty

Gazing only at
The dark
Outside these things
Is light
And joy
And family aching
With the pain of it all
But that armour holds him in
Keeps his head the fixed
And motionless
Struggling to breathe
And he cannot see them yet
These things that come in threes
They say
In threes in cowardice
So as to make victory complete
But we will take our knives
And we will take our tin openers
And we will take our hands and
Hammers
And we'll will cut and hit
Scrape and kick
And push and bite and claw
Until our fingers are worn
And bloody
Until we reach the boy within
Until we peel back
The walls within
And then he will be free
And then he will be him.

# PEACOCK AVENUE

Make your way down Peacock Avenue,
Catch the sunshine on the corner,
Hold tight your breath as you draw closer
to all you know and hate and loathe.
Here on the corner meeting Hope Street,
Cast your eyes on scenes of hate,
I saw the theft of all I longed for,
When you moved to where you are.
Boys and girls will play their games here,
They throw stones and jump their ropes,
Pretty girl that wanders past you,
Dressed in all your torn up hopes.
You'll see a child there speak a mantra,
"I won't live here for all my life."
Steal a smile as you homeward wander,
Remember when you spoke those words.
Trapped for always on this avenue,
Let the sun berate your head,
You are here for all of always,
And always will this be your home

# GRIND

Harsh beats pulse
I ingest
I twitch
Involuntarily start to move
Hard bass shaking the air
Stale sweat lingers
Teeth start to grind
I raise my arms
And flow
Make wild shapes
Eyes tightly closed
Bright light scatter on my face
With a noise like thunder
Unified
We roar
And in my small space
Encapsulated by my ferocious attitude
I rule.

# DENNIS

With no lines around his eyes
Or downturned corners of the mouth
With tunes that can ignite you
Drink is taken to excess because
We are young and he can
With unguarded laughter
at a joke that
Only he knows he struts
Beside the decks - fearless
Careless - no worries for the
Things the
Later seasons may bring
Encapsulated by a roaring
Beat that shuffles into places
That no one thought to go
Where we all needed though
To be
He raises his head
Tilts sideways
And he smiles
And drops a final beat.

# A FORTY-YEAR-OLD HEART

You cannot stop
A forty-year-old heart
That beats and pounds
With strength like this
You cannot yield to it
The fear that envelopes
And blinds completely
Safe here in knowing
All that may be may not be
Reality can be
Always
Held back and imprisoned
Jointly by
Our mutual feeling
Honestly
No one will see

When or if this day
ends and the sun
Sets lightly on
Us. Then just know
This and remember us
Forget the ephemeral ending
Forget all of this fragility but
Remember this strength
Remember

Us
Just that
Just us
Our hands in the others hands
At the start of us and here now
And with a whisper
And a fragile smile
And your head tilted
And with the strength I give you
My last gift
Say goodbye

# HERE – ON THE HILL

A grey man on the mountain hides
The path so often trod
These precipices railed by towers
Of ancient timeworn stones
That through his troublesome weaving
Of his ancient endless beard
Offer no protection
A weeping woman rolls fat
And angry tears along the way
Where we were always surefooted
Now tumble, breathe sharply inward
And grasp at each other
In a cotton clad room of games
Children vie and battle
Sparks and static fly and briefly light the way
Then fade
They only show that
We are deceived
This is not the path we chose
We are lost
We are afraid
Here
Cold and alone
Here - on the hill.

# THE BREATH THAT HAS NO BROTHER

This final moment hung
In the air - it
Does not linger or wait
The finality of the moment
Is over and too soon
The moments before
That escalated
And accelerated with
Undue haste then
Slowed
And turned shallow
Like heels dragging
On an endlessly uphill
Hike. Made harder
By the fog that fell
The eyes grown milky
And unfocused
Till now - this moment
When it arrives and
Has no company
This breath that has no brother.

# LET THEM

Let them be alone just for a while
Hold up the traffic and pause the skies
Make fearful thunder be quiet and bowed
Voices that are usually raised be whispers
Let them stay there in the moment and
Be alone just for a while
Too soon it will all begin - a wall or dam
Will breach and the world will come
Like a brutish man drunkenly forcing his way in
Crashing and thumping and not caring
It will move on like the sea - gripping them in unforgiving tides.
Rolling and roiling and thrashing
one will be deep in the whirlpool of their lives
Tossed and thrown and battered senseless.
By well-wishers. By family. By friends.
Inch by inch and with every beat of
A broken heart - the distance will grow.
The other will float just away - So for now Just for a while - Let
them be alone.

# THESE SILLY NOTES

He used to leave her notes
Scribblings on the back of envelopes
Or shopping lists
Scattered around their home
And in the car
Blinking in the sun
She'd pull down the visor
Only to see a smiley face
On a post it with the words
Love you lots
Or open a kitchen drawer
Rattling it impatiently due to the
Stuck spoon
Thrusting things aside looking for
The right knife or spoon
She'd see a crumpled bit of paper
Smudged ink that stained her skin
Impatiently unfolding it she'd
See the words
Hello beautiful
Waiting for an Uber
On the raining streets of town
When two had cancelled already
Where cars were splashing by
And she was growing cold and sober
She would put her shivering hands in
Her pockets and pull out a folded card
Stuck in the lining

She'd read the words
Ring me if you need picking up x
He didn't tell her how he felt
How some days when she was
Not there
That it was like the world had
Faded into monochrome
That sounds were dull and monotone
That he didn't feel
Like he was not real
He only left her notes
He could not say the words
Arriving home from a trip away
After harsh words has been given
But not received
Never received
She draws a deep and weary breath
On the front door a note
I'm sorry
With a sad not smiling face
Walking past it she moves into
The living room and sees
It's just too hard
I'm no good
In a shaky hand
But hears no voice
And feels no welcome home
Again, she walks by and
Into the kitchen
She reaches for a glass
And sees the last words
He ever wrote
Still full of love
Still bursting with adoration
And care
Words to aid and protect

The glass slips
The glass shatters
Her reflection caught
In the glass for ever
She reaches for the phone
As she reads
The final note
Phone the police
Don't look in the garage

# TOMS BOAT

My single bed was sometimes a wooden boat,
My open window in the summer
Gusted in my curtain, my billowing sail.
My grey and tattered one eyed bear, my captain.
'Onwards boy', he roars and points
At the furious sea – my faded rug
Advancing on we laugh
As the spray spatters our salt-rimed faces,
An adventure every night.
A broken branch my silver sword
As I prepare to repel all boarders.
Our cargo is my pillow, a handsome bag of swag
That all pirates crave
My good ship Dreamer and my captain
We fear no villains nor sea monsters.
From the gap behind the bed head
Where all things fall and don't return
Where all my toys will end up
A terrible kraken roars and rises
We tremble and raise anchor
Afraid of what may come
A thudding draws nearer and
Shaking we huddle down
A blinding light burns our eyes
An angry voice bids us sleep
And obediently I lay down
The turbulent sea becomes a carpet
My battle-scarred captain just a tattered bear

My fine ship Dreamer just a bed once more.
But I am happy.
I am happy

# SUNDAY BEST

Vigorous whispers ululate around the room,
Every lady present feels constrictions in her womb,
Kisses are offered as comfort, the men shake their heads,
But I am suddenly alone, when I learn that you are dead.
We had not spoken for years, but I still felt something break
Inside of me, the pieces fell, and I reached; started for the door,
Afraid that it was true and that I would see you nevermore.
Pinpricks hastened to my eyes, and I feel a sting,
The barb that you placed in my heart,
If there were such a thing, a single tear
more weightier that platinum or gold
falls slowly to the carpet that I can see below.
Then suddenly the hushed silence ends,
And life seems to re-start,
So, angrily, I leave the room,
With the pieces of my heart.
Outside the room, I feel a breeze that burns across my skin,
I can feel the pain of you, and all we would begin,
Inside the room, the volume grows, and voices are all raised,
And fruitlessly the people start at drowning out your name.
(But that is what is on their lips,
Not buried in their minds,
They are afraid so hide their grief,
They are not unkind.)
Your barb that lies within my heart,
Brings about a pause, and in the moment
I see your face, a sob dies in my throat,
And whilst, inside, the world goes on, fondly, I recall

All the joy we would have had, before you chose to fall.
I know that time will bury you, somewhere in my past,
But at this moment, stood outside the world,
I remember everything, and anything,
Just simply to keep you near.
I prayed that you would hold back death,
Keep far from his cold grip,
But as you danced away from him.
Now far away from me.
You fell from the world, my dear, you did not fall from grace,
Painfully, the world goes on, I still dream of your face

# HOUSE OF PAIN

house of pain
home again.
tell us lies,
love dies.
cut the chord
bring us near
cost of life
far too dear
house of lies
travel free
close your eyes
let us be
taught the way
shown how to play
trying hard
not today
turned away
door is closed
tricky concept
no one knows
father figure
growing bigger
blocks the light
every night
Thief of years
(pain giver)
Hope taker
Heart breaker

Dark house
Loveless place
Never tell
of Hidden face
love taken
given fear
night whispers
drawing near
where
we are
wherefrom we came
house of pain
come again

# WHERE DRAGONS SLEEP

Below the un-respected deep,
I spied a place where dragons sleep,
I tasted of their painful skin,
Their ancient eyes where I fell in.
I tried to hide beneath the waves,
Whilst their gaze my face did spy,
From timeless slumber did they rouse,
Around me did the dragons crowd.
Respectfully I tried to flee,
Return from where I came,
Then slowly did their wings unfurl,
Then they called for my name.
Impatiently they glowered on,
Removed me from the light,
They smiled a cruel knowing smile,
There daring me to fight.
My eyes took in this fearful scene,
Was this how I would die?
Devoured by the dragon deep,
Beneath the waves I'd lie.
They took me still despite my pleas,
No hint of mercy nor of care,
I stay there still with wings unfurled,
And wait till you come there

# OUR CHEMICAL REACTION

I fell tripping into her mind
Searching for where she can hide,
Hidden from the sun and doubt
Longing for to get her out.
Ingested by the swollen stream
Suddenly we start to dream.
Crescendo building from one note.
Bonded here, a sense of hope.
Loud colours burst across the scene
Kaleidoscopic scenic dreams.
Course through her heart and mind and eyes
Meteoric diamond skies.
Scorching heat that marks our skin
As we entwine and our lips meet.
Explosive charges from her eyes,
Engulf me whole so I may die.
Hands outstretched across the void
An empty place but filled with noise,
And pumping through my heart and veins
Poisoned blood that kills the grey.
Our matter fades and starts to die,
Entropic forms that caged us in.
Spirit - free, no form or shape,
Free to fly the dream landscape.
Then just too soon we are reclaimed,
Curtain Close and Music End.

Crash landed now - She's Hers. I'm Mine.
Until I fly another time.

# ON A BENCH
# THERE IS A BOY

On a bench
In a park
Sits a boy holding a book
Eating an apple
Letting the wind
Turn the pages.
In the book
There Is a girl
She is running
Down a road
Weeping in the night.
In the road
There is a horse
Gently scraping at
The ground
As the moon
Flies by
Under the moon
There is an ocean
Troubled by the
Tides and battered by
The breeze
In the ocean
There is a boat
Heading to the shore
On the boat there is a man

All he longs for is
To hold her
And to see again her face
In her face
Is a reflection
In the corner of her eye
Of a dresser in
The corner
Holding pictures
Of their life
In the picture
There is a boy
With a book
Lay in his hands
With an apple to
His lips he
Lets the wind
Turn the page.

# HOW I WANT TO BE
# REMEMBERED

When I die and leave the world
Say nothing but the kindest words
"He was kind and loved his friends,
He loved us all until the end."
Say how loved my life had been,
Say I lived out all my dreams.
Say you all will mourn my passing,
With tearful eyes and grief amassing.
I will watch you as you weep,
Take care of you whilst you sleep,
Cover you with goodly light,
If you will mourn me in the night.
Forget that I was weak as man,
I wouldn't do all that man can,
Forget the fact that I could hate,
And spread the tale:
"His heart was great."
Deny the thoughts of how I killed
The love that left me unfulfilled.
Ignore the tale of my slow fall,
instead proclaim
"This man walked tall."
Canonise my memory,
And tell the world how I could be,
Not the truth which could cause pain,
Instead, please elevate my name.

Think of me in better ways
Not how I lived in my last days,
Say my name then wipe a tear,
Say
"I wish that he was here."
When I die and leave the world
Say nothing but the kindest words,
"He loved us all, love
d me, loved you."
Although you know this isn't true

# I SAW A BEAST
# CLIMB IN A TREE

I saw a beast climb into a tree.
I do not think that it saw me.
I called its name and clawed its eyes.
I do not think I saw it die.
The music sang and colours flew. I did not know just what to do.
A flower died. Its petals moved.
The beast and I began to groove.
We danced around the desert sky and angels came to see who'd die.
I hoped and hoped it would be me.
Released from here, it couldn't be.
For night and day, we battled on.
The angels came and then were gone.
My clothes were torn, and I was nude.
The beast then smiled and paused for food.
A devil came and sat to see.
He waited for what we both would be.
A change was coming. I don't know where.
I was so tired; I did not care.
Then suddenly, I felt quite sick.
This had to end and end real quick.
As if the fight had not begun, the beast then left then there was one.
I looked around and jumped quite high. Against all hope I didn't die.
The devil smiled and crouched right down.

I held my breath. He laughed then frowned.
"Your time has come" the devil said.
Before I knew it, I was dead.
I slumber now beneath the ground
and there I lie and make no sound.
One day I'll come and fight again.
Until then I stay the same.

# A WALTZ

I feel her coming closer now,
I see her waltz away,
I sense her drawing closer still
Just fingertips away.
Enticing me, enraptured we
Dance and almost touch,
I nearly feel her in my arms,
I want this very much.
I see her perfect frame spin round,
Her smile is drawing near,
Eyes closed, I stretch to touch her lips,
Too soon, She disappears.

# EPHEMERAL

So let it burn
And fade
Ignite it with a brilliant spark
And retreat
Watch it coruscate from the edges in
Drawing near
It will flare and shine
Look away
Soon it will lift
And fly
Growing dimmer and lighter
Far away
You'll watch and stare and squint
Long after
Wondering what it was and where
Did it go.

# THE SURGEON

If I could
Then I would
Cut out the
Weight lay in
Your fragile heart
With a scalpel
Bright and clean
I would begin
Masked and robed
Harsh lights blinding
I would start
Here and now
Cut the skin
Expose the heart
Excise the weight
Remove the pain
And the sorrow
Take it all
And then subsume
Place it within
My endless heart
And then with
My shaking hands
I would close
With fine thread
And shining needle
And close your
Wound leaving nothing

But a subtle scar
I would take
It all within
Leaving you whole
If I could
Then I would
I truly would
Be the surgeon
Of your heart.

# WHEN THE WAVES GREW STILL

When the waves grew still
And becalmed we float
In circles
Afraid to break the silence
That oppresses us
These words need saying
Though. The stars that
Once lit our way and
Guided us seem
Foreign now. These are
Stranger skies to us and
With no clear route or
Maps we float
These waves grew still
And becalmed and starved
Of bravery
With weakling voices
Unable to elaborate
We float here
In awkward heavy
Growing silence.

# INSOMNIA

can't sleep - black night
every fold hurts me
and digging in my skin
mornings drawing in
so tired - and wired
tossing in the sea
sweat dries on my skin
mornings drawing in
eyes hurt - feel heavy
I cannot make them close
tomorrow don't begin
but mornings drawing in
sun rise - I hate you
seasick as I toss and roll
crying as I see the sun
morning has begun

05:44:35 am

# ME, REFLECTED

I gaze into my mirror,
And looking back I see,
A sad and weary lonely man.
I have denied the God in me
Bent double by my doubts
Imprisoned by my fears,
Small comfort when I look at me
and my reflected tears.
If I were to smash this mirror
How would I live then?
If I should die, would I be free
To live my life again ?

# MARRY/SNOG/AVOID

SO come on and be YOURSELF
kiss him. kiss him HARDER
liberating isn't it but it
only gets harder
(ask him go on ask him)
he'll tell you that its HARDER
Go on and move with him
syncopation is ATTRACTIVE
to him ALONE he wants to see you move
Blow his mind away scratch him SLOW
just to see if he admires you
If you are ready LET HIM KNOW
Don't let yourself down - show him what you NEED
If he won't GIVE it cut him to the quick
If he is BLEEDING, then bandage all his wounds
So will you kiss him. Kiss him SLOW
Dance with him slower. MAKE his garden grow.
If you are angry PULL off his scabs and make him BLEED
If you are lucky, He will give YOU what you NEED.
Don't TRY to teach him - He SHOULD know this on his OWN
So can you see how the MIGHTY thing has grown
Its not so mighty when he is IN BED alone
With just the CONCEPT and the smell of your PERFUME
So, see him fumble and SPILL HIS SEED on fallow ground
Go on and ask him to LAY you. Beg him to SLAY you.
See if he will PLAY you.
REGALE you. SAIL You. IMPALE you.
FAIL you or NAIL YOU - The choice is YOURS alone.

# I WAS THERE

first I was there
then I was not there
I came
I saw
I lived then died.
I know you did not care.
I saw no tears
only fears
and your angry gaze
was cast around
and you; distressed
wondered who would be next.
when I was laid here
six feet down
"they cried"
they said
for me deceased
but looking up
I only saw relief
on all your ageing faces
I saw your lonely ends
in many different places
and I, not distressed
wonder who will be next.

# JUST A FATHER
# PART TWO

You are a crinkled smile
A pair of twinkling eyes
The smell of new wood freshly planed
You're the sound of doors opening
And the scent of caramel late at night
Secretly eaten under covers.
You are lilting laughter
Scattered like rain drops
You are a symbol and an aim
A thing to measure by
You are the soft breeze that blows by
As the swing that is pushed rises
And falls
The taste of sweet confectionary
On a weekend
You are the feel of paper robots
And the sound of scratching ballpoint pens
You are a scribbled note left on
The kitchen top that says
'Gone to the flicks'
And the diesel smell of orange buses
You're the strength it takes
To lift someone in the air
You are a thought and a memory
That's clear
And crisp

Bright and enduring
And one that doesn't fade
You are just a father
And I am just your son.

# ALL MY CHAPTER ONES

# CHAPTER ONE

The village where I live is quiet and small - there is barely any traffic, and the birds sing throughout the year. No one flies south for the winter here.

You can leave your front door and throw a loop around it within an hour - although not many people do.

Along the main road there are a number of shops - the kind of places owned and run by people who do it for a hobby. Sometimes, when you go in, you feel like you're intruding.

Most of our villagers seem to be retired - that or their lottery numbers came up some years ago. The younger end tend to work outside the village.

On a crisp spring morning you can see them walking - their lunches packed and smiles on their faces - and heading for the bus or the train.

As the light falls and the ground softens - you'll see them walking back home. Squinting in the half light and with a little less joy and a little more fatigue about them. Like a kind of weariness maybe.

Sometimes you can see them - it's almost imperceptible- slowing a little as they near home. It's as though they're mentally preparing themselves for being at home.

It's not - I think - that they don't want to be there. It's never that - it's more that they know that life is waiting for them there - real life which doesn't ebb or slow. It's constant and so they need to be ready.

At the weekend there's a quieter air about our village. People are slow to rise - unless they're runners or cyclists. They get up, blinking away the dreams and sleep from their eyes - they slowly meander downstairs and carelessly flop in front of the tv.

For some there might be a nice moment of peace before the rest of their world awakens. They might sit and talk with a pet - ruffling their fur and tickling their backs.

Before long, others might join them, and they could share a warm drink. For those with children the day will start earlier. They could be up with the athletes of the village preparing endless choices of breakfast for the ones they love who don't know what they want - only that it's not that.

The runners and the cyclists will have been up for hours already. They choose the solitary life of endless laps of the local hills and paths. They might fly down the canal and follow its undulations and weaving winding route to the next village.

They likely stop there, impatiently waiting for the local cafe to open its doors - where they'll enjoy a virtuous and sinless meal. Having eaten they'll return to the road or paths and make their way home - albeit slightly slower. With bellies full and their minds emptied they'll be ready for the day.

# CHAPTER ONE

There is a house with painted windows that backs onto a beach. It is tall and wooden and has a porch that faces the sea. On the porch there is a light that flickers all day and all night.

On the veranda there is a small metal seat for two. It is rusting and fragile. The cushions were once bright colours but have faded in the constant sunlight to a faint mixture of grey and brown.

There are small steps that are uneven and rotten in places. Chipped and peeling paint surrounds the windows and the door.

The windows are smeared with sand and there are hanging baskets either side of the door. The plants are not well tended and are in need of water.

You can swim up to the beach and be dry by the time you reach the doorway. The door is never locked and is always ajar.

In the day light the house is welcoming. The shutters are always open, and the blinds are always raised. Music can often be heard playing from within.

As the night falls and the stars emerge, it becomes less so. Wrapped in shadows and shorn of its deceits by the star light, it is forbidding. Strangers that walk along the beach may pause, and peer at the house and then, feeling uneasy, walk on.

As the night closes in and the temperature falls, there is a stillness only interrupted by the buzzing and flickering of the lights on the porch. The soft pitta-patta on the edge of hearing signifies the arrival of the moths.

These blind and fluttering clumsy creatures collide endlessly with the light that they are drawn to. Like the ghosts of butterflies, wreathed in smoky light they batter against the bulb. Like dancers on a stage in a show that never ends.

The house cools as the light dims. It's creaking crackling settles like a whisper. It is as though the house is sighing or relaxing. There's comfort in the night.

Eventually the whispering deceits and shadows of the house begin to fade as the sun starts to rise.

Slowly, the sun touches the sand. It edges onwards. It strikes the bottom step.

You could hear the sounds of a city waking - the grumbling of cars and the yowling of cats - they can be heard in the distance, stretching and shuddering and readying to race for food. Motors rev and churn whilst faint voices are raised in greeting to friends and strangers.

Inside the house, something stirs. The door begins to open.

A small and clumsy man blinks in the low sunlight and looks around. It's still early - the world is still waking - so there is little for him to see. Someone still satisfied, he straightens his glasses and closes the door without looking behind.

His clothes are not matched, and his hair is crumpled - he's dressed like a blind thief. Still somehow there is some dignity about him - covered though in a veil of disregard.

He scratched his chin and pulls closed his jacket and walks away, coughing as he goes.

# CHAPTER ONE

t could be called AnyTown. It's the kind of place that people travel from rather than to. Thirty minutes, tops from the city. Still its light-years and decades apart. It's called Glossop and for now, it's home.

It's a town like your town, a place of grief and shadows. You can walk the street on any given day; do the weekly Friday night tour of the pubs after work and never see its underbelly. There are people who live there who could change the world if they wanted. People who should never see the light of day.

It's incestuous too. Boys are passed from girl to girl and girls from boy to boy then back again. Like any town, there comes a point where you just can't breathe any more. The passing strangers are closer and closer, hemming you in till all you can see are your mistakes. Your regrets. The wish you hadn'ts and the if only you hads.

Growing closer to the point of no return, you wear your mask gripped tightly to your skin. You only face people head on because that's all you know how to do.

Like horny dogs on heat, you rut and fight and sweat and swear, looking for a way out. Looks hard and that's what counts. In public anyway.

Alone? Well, that's a different story. The sweat, the fear, the certainty that there's something more and the greater certainty that you'll never see it.

When you were small and the world was simpler, then life was easier. You had a mum. You had a dad. A brother too. There you were, stood in the road (probably wearing that policeman helmet; it was never off your head), snot on your face and dirt on your knees.

Facing the day with a smile each day. A smile that could light up strangers faces like a pinball machine on tilt. It dimmed, though. Life does that.

It starts to press lightly on your shoulders. A tiny bit more each day, adding to the load. Just unnoticeable. But it grows. Gets heavier. Pushes at the lights in your eyes till one day they're snuffed and all you can think about is the weight.

There's always a chance you think. A little respite. You know you shouldn't, but you can't help it. Rubbing the sleep from the corners of your eyes you lift your head which has grown so heavy. You glance up.

In the distance you can see the towers of the nearest city. There's only one way out of here and even that only gives temporary escape.

Stitched tightly into this tapestry you know you'll be drawn back eventually. So, you put your head down, pull up your hood to hold back the endless rain and walk the hill.

Breaking into a short and breathless jog, you arrive at the station. In amidst the commuters and the students stood with bleary pin hole eyes you see them.

They're not your brothers, not really. Not by blood anyway. But they're the only ones who ever stood by you. They're more family than anyone else.

Holding back a smile at this simple joy (because it's just not cool, yeah), you nod, each into your pocket for your tobacco and rizlas and nod.

'Lads', you say. 'Town, then?'

# CHAPTER ONE

So then. Nothing ever starts, does it? Things happen, people change, the sun comes up and goes down again. It all just happens, whether we want it to or not. You can read as many books as you like but when they open with 'and this is how it began' or something similar, then call BS.

It doesn't start then; we're just jumping on the back of the bus at that point.

The fact is that when you're feeling a story, you're taught to start with something arresting. To grab the readers eye and draw them in. An opening paragraph is a sales pitch; nothing more.

But (there's always a but – just more sales stuff isn't it) there's this. Any story needs to be one thing only. It needs to be true. It might be set in space, or it might be set on another planet, that doesn't matter.

When I say it has to be true, I am not being literal. I mean that when you read the story you believe in it. You have to care what happens. When you get to the last page and you close the book, you should know in your bones that it was true. You should ache with the truth of it.

The lives you read about were real. The things they did or didn't do all mattered. The story made you care.

That's a big ask of any writer. Scares most of them shitless to be blunt. So often they'll shy away from it. Make light of the story. Mock the people in it. Try and be too smart. It's the difference between a good story and a great one, isn't it?

Like I said way back up there, nothing ever starts. The world and everyone one on it (even those still unborn) are on an endless bus ride down the widest and most convoluted road you can imagine.

We, as readers, choose to jump on board as it slows by our stop, and watch and listen for a while. We watch and listen, and we care.

The bus is slowing down. It's pulling into our stop. The door is sliding open. We can, if we choose, hop on board to join the story.

The bus pulls away with some of us on board. As the darkness clears and the smell of diesel fades, we blink and look at where we are and what we can see.

So, there's these lads on a train platform.

# CHAPTER ONE

There is a funny little village in the North of England and it is surrounded by hills. All of the hills have strange names.

There is Indians Head. If you squint and cross your eyes a bit, it looks a little bit like a red Indian chief wearing a big head dress. If you are ever there you should look up. If it isn't too foggy, then cross your eyes a bit and look up. You just might see him.

There is Dovestones and there is Pots and Pans. At the top of Pots and Pans there is a big stone carving that was put there to remember all the boys and girls who went away to fight in a big war.

This is very sad. These boys and girls weren't much older than you, but they went far away with tin hats on and guns in their hands and they fought. They didn't really know how to fight but they knew that they should.

They knew that if they didn't, some bad men would come and hurt everyone that they loved. Some of them were lucky and they came home. Some of them were a little less lucky and came home but without all their arms and legs.

Some of them didn't come home at all. They died where they fought. These boys and girls are why once a year, everyone goes up to the big stone to be quiet and to think and to remember. They remember the children who never grew up.

If you walk down the big hill you will come to a road. On the corner of this road is a little school.

It's a very special school.

The teachers are nice, and the children are kind. The food is lovely and everyone who goes there has a happy life. That isn't why it is special though. Lots of schools are like this – I bet your school is just as happy and kind. It could even be happier.

It is special because something wonderful and magical happens here every night after it closes.

Everyone finishes their lessons and packs up their bags and the teachers turn out the classroom lights. They then take the children to the playground to wait for their mums and dads to pick them up. When everyone has gone home, the teachers pack up their books and go to their cars wishing everyone a good evening. The headteacher picks up her hat and coat and puts them on.

If it is cold, then she might put on her scarf and gloves as well. She knows it's important to wrap up warm when it's winter. She locks the front door and then goes to her car.

She might look around the car park to make sure that everyone has gone home. She will smile. Then she'll drive away and leave the school in darkness till the next day.

Now the school is dark and locked and closed, you might be wondering why and how anything magical can happen.

Well it can, and it does. I know because I walked past one night in winter. There was a lot of snow on the ground and the roads were very icy. I had to leave my car a few miles away because it was so dangerous.

I had my big coat on and my hat (remember, you should always wrap up warm in winter), but I didn't have my wellingtons on, so I was slipping around all over. I had been walking for about an hour and a half and I was very tired. Walking in deep snow is a lot harder than walking when there is no snow.

I had fallen over at least two or three times already and was very tired. In the distance, I could see the twinkling lights of the houses and I knew I wasn't far from home. My breath made clouds like a dragon blowing smoke and there was ice on my beard.

I looked up and I could see all the stars in the sky. It was very beautiful.

When I stopped for a rest, I leant on a railing, so I wouldn't fall over. The wind was blowing and whooping around me, but I thought I could hear something.

Well two things.

I was certain I could hear children laughing. I was almost certain I could hear a dog barking and yipping.

I felt very confused because I knew the school was closed so I thought I had better have a look.

I left my railing and walked a few unsteady steps to the school. Where it should have been in darkness, I could see a light in one of the classrooms. I could hear laughter.

So, I scraped the ice from the window with my glove and I peeked in. I couldn't believe what I could see.

# CHAPTER ONE

You

Ok so there you are. Sat on the bus travelling into town to go to work. It's just another day – same as any other. Looking around you see the same weary faces. There's the guy in the suit that is frayed at the edges. It's seen better times and so has the man wearing it. Mr Clean you call him to yourself. The old lady with the shopping trolley on wheels. She sits there on the seat at the front and looks around smiling at everyone who gets on. No one smiles back. She's Mrs. Pepperpot.

Across from you is a young mum. She's on her mobile clicking and swiping away. The child next to her is stood up and clearly bored. He is drawing in the condensation on the grimy window. He looks around and you smile and nod.

With a cough and a groan, the bus slows up. More folk getting on to go to the town that the world forgot. The doors go psssh and shudder open. Glancing up you see someone new. It's a young lad – can't be more than fifteen or sixteen.

'No school?' you think then dismiss it. It's none of your business. There is though, something about him.

He's got a mass of curly red hair that's clearly not been within any distance of a barber. Must be six foot tall – when did kids get so big, you wonder. His jeans are spattered with paint and are way too short. He's wearing odd socks and his trainers are Adidas 'Wish they were' if you're any judge. God knows, you wore enough of them when you were his age. You can still remember rocking up at school in your trainers and everyone laughing because they had four stripes instead of three. Your mum got them from some dodgy stall on Ashton Market.

He's wearing a hoody that's way too big for him and there's a tear in the pocket. It's seen better times just like Mr Clean. He counts out his money and waves a pass to the driver who clearly couldn't care and who waves him on impatiently.

He wanders down the bus holding on to the seat backs to steady himself and collapses into the seat behind you.

The bus starts to groan as it strains the climb up the hill to the cutting. You love the cutting – it's the only part of your journey that you do. It's childish but it's all about that frog in the wall.

For some reason (you've no clue what) there's a hollowed-out stone in the wall – it's just above head height. Someone paints white every year and then paints a green frog.

You can remember the first time your dad pointed it out to you – on one of the many days you went on trips out to the Peak. "First one to see the frog in the wall", he would say in between coughing and lighting another cigarette.

Shifting in your seat and feeling the thirty-year-old foam offering no protection to your backside you twist round looking for it. It's hard to see through the filth on the windows but you swipe the condensation away and look anyway. Tradition, isn't it, dad?

Arching around, you grip the seat back and twist to see it – making eye contact with the lad with the ginger mop. His face is clean, but his eyes are a shock. They look older than the rest of him.

'Looking for the frog? It's there' he says and points to his right. Just in time you see it and chance a quick smile of thanks.

'Know why it's there?' he says. You shake your head a little – half expecting a dirty joke.

'When they made the cutting, they bust open a stone – and found like a fossil of a frog. They reckon it crawled into a crack and then ate too much and got stuck.'

'Really?', you say. This is, you reckon, likely to be the most interesting thing you are going to hear this week.

'So, they say', he says then breaks eye contact and slumps a bit more in the seat. You're about twenty minutes from the last stop and it looks like he's setting down for a nap on the way. Regardless, you nod your thanks and turn back around to face the front.

Sleeping on a bus. It isn't something you every managed to get the knack of. Too many bad smells – hard seats and people barging into you when they get on and get off. It's either that or someone sitting next to you and trying to take two thirds of the seat that is barely wide enough for one.

You look down at the Kindle in your hand. Every night you charge it, and every single day you sit here on the bus just holding it. You don't even turn it on, never mind turning a page.

You aren't even sure why they bought it for you – it's not like you read a lot. You just don't like to. Maybe they're trying to encourage you – maybe that's it.

It's stories though. The whole thing doesn't make sense to you. Nothing ever starts, does it? Things happen, people change, the sun comes up and goes down again. It all just happens, whether you want it to or not. You can read as many books as you like but when they open with 'and this is how it began' or something similar, then you call bullshit and put it down.

It doesn't start then; we're just jumping on the bus at that point, you think. Heaving at the smell of the diesel fumes, wincing with every bump in the road – we're only just joining the story mid-way. At some point in the journey, you'll ring the bell on the strip in the roof that rarely works and then make your way to the front.

If you're feeling sociable, you might give the driver and nod then get off. The story on the bus still carries on though. That's what gets you about books – what doesn't make sense. That lad behind you didn't appear red-eyed, ginger and fully formed the moment he got on the bus. He was there before then – and he'll be there when he gets off. You have no idea what he'll get up to today and no way of knowing.

You wipe the rheum from your eyes and blink. Twenty minutes till you get to town – where the reek of fuel will be replaced by the smell of just another day. Till home-time. You bet the boy behind you is going to have a more interesting day than you. You think about what his story might be and where it will take him.

You settle in and try to get comfortable. Wondering what your fellow travellers' stories will be.

Alex

Bzzzz Bzzzz

'Can't be the alarm', you think. It feels like you've only been in bed for an hour – tops.

Bzzzz Bzzzz

Yep – it's the alarm. You grope around and flail aimlessly till it stops. With a yawn that could swallow the sun, you gingerly open your eyes and look around. In the corner of your room, the damp paper is still peeling off to show the crumbling plaster and lath underneath. The poster of Doctor Who is falling down and failing to cover the cracks.

You cough – a deep booming cough that is larger than the chest it comes from. You look down at your body. A greyish skin wraps around ribs that you can count. You've kicked off the blanket in the night, so your morning glory is poking up, loud and proud. Briefly, you consider having a wank then dismiss the thought.

Later on, you think. Maybe when I get in, and mums asleep.

Thing is, she may as well be asleep for all the talking she does. You can hear her clattering around in the kitchen making herself yet another brew. That's about all she does, these days – well as long as you can remember, if you're being honest.

Drinks tea and cries when she thinks no one can hear her. It's not her fault, you know – life has been a bit shit for her since dad died. The thing is, you think – it's not yours either.

Anyway. You shuffle up in the bed and rub your eyes – trying to ease yourself into full alert. Your window doesn't have a curtain, just an old sheet hung over it – through the gaps where the nails have torn through, you can see that it's still dark outside.

Abruptly, you sit up and swivel round to sit on the side of the bed. The action makes you feel a bit dizzy, but you shake it off and think about today's plans. It's the same old thing really – it's Saturday and Saturday means town. You'll be meeting the lads and getting on the train into Manchester. Glossop to town – 35 minutes dead on. Bit of a mooch around the Arndale and the Corn Exchange – bite to eat then home. It's standard with you and your boys.

You've lost wood now, so it's safe to get up, you think. You yank on your tracksuit from yesterday which reeks of day-old cigarettes but is otherwise clean. You kick your feel into your snide trainers. Stumbling to the door, you push and hear it creak open and make a visit to the bathroom then down to the kitchen.

'Morning, mum', you say as you sit down. "Fancy a brew?'

Nothing. She's stood at the window again just staring. That mug of tea in her hand will be cold before she takes another mouthful you reckon.

She's only 40 but she looks so much older. Every hardship she's suffered is carved in lines on her skin – literally. You can see the marks on her arms that are from the night that no one talks about. Her hair is greasy and pulled back into a ponytail. She gives a sigh that is almost a sob and turns round.

'Morning, ginger nut' she says and tries her hardest to smile. It almost looks real. 'I've been thinking about your dad again', she says.

You've no idea what to say to that, it's all she ever says to you really. So, you just nod and reach over to flick the kettle on.

Whilst it's boiling, you sit and wait. The longer you spend in this house, the harder it is to breath. The smaller the rooms seem to you. It's as though the house which used to be a home is slowly closing in and crushing you. It wraps around your head and chest and constricts slowly. Your breaths come quicker and shallower – like they did when you were told what had happened to dad – like you're hardly breathing at all. Tighter and quicker and harder to swallow.

The walls move closer in nearer and nearer until it's like you're in a suit of armour. The helmet has come down and it feels like it's never coming off again. All you can see is there through the tiny slit – and all you can see is your mum. Mum who wishes she'd died eleven years ago, who in a way did die then. She's never going to be happy, never going to be normal and never going to be the mum you want or need.

Your chest is hurting, and you can hear the blood in your veins pumping and flowing and rushing – you look around in every direction but still all you can see is her.

You're almost panicking but then the reverie is broken by the kettle clicking off – so you stand and make a brew. Tea with three and loads of milk. You drink it down in one and turn to your mum.

Without making eye contact, you mumble and stutter.

'Off out' you say and gently close the door behind you without waiting for a reply.

Once outside you can breathe normally. Sucking in big gusty gasps of air, you walk down the path and vault the gate. Hang a left in the ginnel and head for the bus stop.

Just in time, you see the 237 chuntering towards you lit by the pale and barely yellow streetlights. You hold out your hand to call the bus and remember you've left your fags in your room.

As you make your way down the bus to a seat, holding on to the rails to steady yourself you look around at the other passengers and sit behind the guy with the kindle.

# CHAPTER ONE

I had a shave tonight. I ran the water till it was almost too hot to touch and then splashed it on my face to soften the grey and brown bristles.

As I lathered up the foam, I thought a heard a noise behind me - and I looked around.

As I looked back to the mirror and saw my ageing face reflected, I gave a small shudder. Involuntary really.

Something wasn't right. With my reflection.

—-

Didn't sleep so well. I've woken up after eventually drifting into a light doze. All I keep thinking about is last night. Try to air sense of it I guess.

My reflection in the mirror. It just seemed odd - I can't say why but it wasn't correct.

My eyes are droopy these days - my wife comments on it all the time. But not in the mirror. There was a vibrancy and a hardness in them.

And that noise! Like a breath or a sigh behind me. Disappointed and resigned in tone. But everyone was asleep. I must have imagined it.

I didn't imagine the slick sheen of sweat on my back and arms. Or how the hair on my nape shifted imperceptibly.

It makes no sense - and I don't know why it preyed on me. I could swear that - it was almost as though - it wasn't me looking back.

—-

Work has been a waste and a joke today. Yes, I've fallen behind - and yes I've been distracted. Mea culpa and so on.

It's the people though! I swear they're treating me differently - like they keep forgetting that I'm there.

I swear - three times today the weirdest things have happened.

Like I do, I nipped into the meeting room to take my lunch. Chicken sub if you're interested. I sat there eating it and Steve came in with a colleague I'd better not name, and they started making out. It got very heavy and heated for a while - me sat there with my mouth open and bits of salad falling out of the sub while they went at it.

This was in full view - like I say - as though I wasn't there.

It wrapped up quickly when they heard a noise outside the door. So that was weird thing one.

In the afternoon, the second thing happened. I was sat tapping away on my keyboard - valiantly trying to catch up on a very overdue code change. Lost in the brackets and maths to be honest. Anyway, a guy came over from sales - looked around to see if anyone was looking - and took my monitor lead!

I was too stunned to speak until he'd gone back to his desk.

I mean - I know I'm here. I can touch things - I shoved Steve a bit before to test that out. Even pinched a biscuit from the kitchen. Odd though.

Thing three didn't really happen at work - more on the way home but I'm tired now. I'll tell you later.

—-

# ABOUT THE AUTHOR

## Christopher M Doyle

I'm a <mutters> 50 odd year old man. Married to Amanda with three children - Sam, Tom and Ruby (my Boo).

I've written poetry most of my life - usually as a cathartic exercise to make sense of the thoughts in my head.

Every poem here was written in one draft, saved and then remains untouched.

Every Chapter One marks the start of a story - unfinished and unreviewed.